1,000,000 Books
are available to read at

Forgotten Books

www.ForgottenBooks.com

Read online
Download PDF
Purchase in print

ISBN 978-1-334-58453-4
PIBN 10771789

This book is a reproduction of an important historical work. Forgotten Books uses state-of-the-art technology to digitally reconstruct the work, preserving the original format whilst repairing imperfections present in the aged copy. In rare cases, an imperfection in the original, such as a blemish or missing page, may be replicated in our edition. We do, however, repair the vast majority of imperfections successfully; any imperfections that remain are intentionally left to preserve the state of such historical works.

Forgotten Books is a registered trademark of FB &c Ltd.
Copyright © 2018 FB &c Ltd.
FB &c Ltd, Dalton House, 60 Windsor Avenue, London, SW19 2RR.
Company number 08720141. Registered in England and Wales.

For support please visit www.forgottenbooks.com

1 MONTH OF FREE READING

at

www.ForgottenBooks.com

By purchasing this book you are eligible for one month membership to ForgottenBooks.com, giving you unlimited access to our entire collection of over 1,000,000 titles via our web site and mobile apps.

To claim your free month visit:
www.forgottenbooks.com/free771789

* Offer is valid for 45 days from date of purchase. Terms and conditions apply.

English
Français
Deutsche
Italiano
Español
Português

www.forgottenbooks.com

Mythology Photography **Fiction**
Fishing Christianity **Art** Cooking
Essays Buddhism Freemasonry
Medicine **Biology** Music **Ancient Egypt** Evolution Carpentry Physics
Dance Geology **Mathematics** Fitness
Shakespeare **Folklore** Yoga Marketing
Confidence Immortality Biographies
Poetry **Psychology** Witchcraft
Electronics Chemistry History **Law**
Accounting **Philosophy** Anthropology
Alchemy Drama Quantum Mechanics
Atheism Sexual Health **Ancient History**
Entrepreneurship Languages Sport
Paleontology Needlework Islam
Metaphysics Investment Archaeology
Parenting Statistics Criminology
Motivational

Lewisham Antiquarian Society.

Twelfth Annual Report

Rules,
List of Officers and Members,
Balance Sheet,
and
Publications of the Society.

Printed for the Society by
Charles North, Blackheath Printing Works, S.E.

1897.

Contents.

	PAGE
LIST OF OFFICERS AND MEMBERS OF THE COUNCIL ...	vii
TWELFTH ANNUAL REPORT	viii
BALANCE SHEET	x
PROCEEDINGS, 1894–1896	xi
RULES	xii
LIST OF MEMBERS	xiii–xvi
PUBLICATIONS OF THE SOCIETY	xvii
ON THE DERIVATION AND MEANING OF THE NAME "LEWISHAM." BY THE REV. PROFESSOR W. W. SKEAT, LITT.D., &c.	3, 4
ON THE INFLUENCE OF THE CRUSADES UPON ENGLISH ARCHITECTURE. BY JOSEPH W. BROOKES	5–19

Lewisham Antiquarian Society.

President:
PERCY W. AMES, Esq., F.S.A.

Vice-Presidents:
H. E. ARMSTRONG, Esq., F.R.S., Ph.D.
E. W. BRABROOK, Esq., F.S.A., P.A.I.
Canon RHODES BRISTOW, M.A.
Sir JOHN FARNABY LENNARD, Bart., F.S.A.
T. V. HOLMES, Esq., F.G.S.
Rev. BROOKE LAMBERT, B.C.L., M.A.
Right Rev. The LORD BISHOP OF LICHFIELD, D.D.
Sir JOHN LUBBOCK, Bart., M.P., F.R.S., F.L.S.
Sir SPENCER MARYON MARYON-WILSON, Bart.
Right Hon. The EARL OF NORTHBROOK, G.C.S.I.

Hon. Secretaries and Treasurers:
LELAND L. DUNCAN, Esq., F.S.A., Rosslair, Lingards Road.
HERBERT C. KIRBY, Esq., Linden Villa, Lewisham Park.

Auditor:
JOSEPH DEWICK, Esq.

Council:
JAMES S. BAIN, Esq.
WILLIAM E. BALL, Esq., LL.D.
Rev. SAMUEL BICKERSTETH, M.A.
CHARLES A. BRADFORD, Esq.
JOSEPH W. BROOKES, Esq.
WILLIAM HODGETTS, Esq.
HERBERT JONES, Esq., F.S.A.
FRED. MOTE, Esq., LL.B., M.A.
EDWARD H. OXENHAM, Esq., F.R.S.L.
R. GARRAWAY RICE, Esq., F.S.A.
WALTER ROBINS, Esq., B.Sc.
EDWARD C. SINKLER, Esq.

Lewisham Antiquarian Society.

Twelfth Annual Report, 1896.

The Council in presenting the Twelfth Annual Report is glad to be able to congratulate the members on the satisfactory condition of the Society.

During the year the following meetings have been held:—

(1) At Otford on Saturday, 2nd May, 1896. Here the Society was very kindly received by the Rector, Dr. Hunt, who escorted the members through the village to the Parish Church, the ruins of the manor house of the Archbishops of Canterbury, and the well of St. Thomas. Filston Farmhouse, which contains much domestic work of interest, was also visited by kind permission of Mr. Hale, who exhibited several objects found in the neighbourhood.

(2) At Cliffe-at-Hoo and Cooling on Saturday, 6th June, 1896. Here the rectory was visited and described by the Rector, and subsequently the interesting church of St. Helen. At Cooling Castle Mr. Duncan read a short paper at the entrance gate, after which the members inspected the ruins of the Keep, and in the short time available the Parish Church, where the fine arcading in the chancel, the wooden roof, and some benches of Henry VI's time were pointed out by the Rector.

(3) At Swanscombe on Saturday, 15th August, 1896, under the direction of Mr. H. Stopes. The points visited were (i) the spot where the "Galley Hill Skull" was found; (ii) the pits where the majority of the flint implements of the district are obtained; (iii) the Parish Church, interesting from its former association with St. Hildfert, whose shrine stood therein; (iv) Mr. Stopes' own house, which contains an unrivalled collection of flint implements; (v) Swanscombe Wood to see the British Camp and the supposed site of the Roman Station of Vagniacæ.

(4) At Lewisham on Monday, 21st December, 1896, for the exhibition of various objects of interest. These included several views of Lewisham, dated 1770, photographs of early church plate at Bristol, &c., &c. An inventory of the contents of a Lewisham husbandman's house in 1530 was read by Mr. Duncan,

With regard to this last meeting the Council hopes next winter to arrange for several of a similar nature, in order to give those members who have not hitherto taken any active part in the Society's proceedings an opportunity of bringing to notice any matter in which they may be interested.

The Council desires to express its best thanks to the Clergy and others for the facilities given for visiting the various places of interest, and to all those who in any way have assisted in the success of the meetings.

It is with very great regret that the Council has to record the death during the past year of the Rev. Thomas Bramley, D.D. He was the second President of the Society, and his kindly courtesy and ever-ready help contributed not a little to the Society's success at a critical period in its history. Although his departure from this neighbourhood necessitated his resigning the presidential chair, he still remained on the list of Vice-Presidents, and had hoped to welcome the Society to Warwick.

The Society now numbers 152 members. The Balance Sheet shows the financial position of the Society to be satisfactory, and the Council propose to continue the series of publications by printing and issuing to members whose subscriptions have been paid the paper read at the meeting held in January, 1895, by Mr. J. W. Brookes, on "The Influence of the Crusades on Architecture," together with a List of Members and Diary of the Proceedings of the Society since the last volume was printed.

Signed on behalf of the Council,

PERCY W. AMES, *President.*

LELAND L. DUNCAN } *Hon. Secretaries*
HERBERT C. KIRBY } *and Treasurers.*

Lewisham, March, 1897.

Lewisham Antiquarian Society.

Balance Sheet—1st Jan., 1895, to 31st Dec., 1895.

1895.		£	s.	d.	1895.		£	s.	d.
Jan. 1.	Balance in hand ...	10	4	5	Postage and Stationery ...		3	8	9
	81 Subscriptions at 2/6	10	2	6	Lantern Slides			15	0
	Profit on Chelsfield Excursion ...	1	11	2	Hire of Rooms, &c. ...			13	6
	Profit on Malling Excursion ...		1	5	Expenses at Ightham ...			2	7
	Sale of Publications		1	0	Donation—Silchester Excavation Fund		2	2	0
					Printing, per C. North ...		2	0	0
					Dec. 31—Balance carried forward		12	18	8
		£22	0	6			£22	0	6

1896. Jan. 1st—Balance in hand ... £12 18 8

Audited and found correct,

(*Signed*) JOSEPH DEWICK.

Lewisham Antiquarian Society.

Balance Sheet—1st Jan., 1896, to 31st Dec., 1896.

1896.		£	s.	d.	1896.	£	s.	d.
Jan. 1.	Balance in hand ...	12	18	8	Postage and Stationery ...	2	4	0
	64 Subscriptions ...	8	0	0	Donation—Silchester Excavation Fund	2	2	0
	Profit on Otford Excursion ...	1	1	3	Printing, per C. North ...	1	12	3
	Ditto Cliffe-at-Hoo		12	0	Advertisement at Bazaar		12	6
	Ditto Swanscombe	1	0	0	Balance carried forward...	17	3	2
	Sale of Publications		2	0				
		£23	13	11		£23	13	11

1897. Balance in hand ... £17 3 2

Audited and found correct,

16th March, 1897.   (*Signed*) JOSEPH DEWICK.

Diary of Proceedings, 1894-96.

1894.	13th Feb.	Ninth General Meeting, in the hall of Colfe's Grammar School, and Paper by Rev. T. BRAMLEY, D.D., on the Guilds of England, illustrated from the published History of the Leathersellers' Company.
	3rd April.	Meeting at St. Mary's National Schools.—Paper by LELAND L. DUNCAN, Esq., F.S.A., on the Head Masters of the Colfe's Grammar School (afterwards printed).—Exhibition of views of some old Lewisham houses, &c.
	5th May.	Meeting at Sevenoaks; the Parish Church and Knole House visited.
	26th May.	Visit to Darenth, Horton Kirby, and Farningham Parish Churches.
	16th June.	Meeting at Titsey, under G. LEVESON-GOWER, Esq., V.P.S.A.
	4th July.	Meeting at Silchester, under HERBERT JONES, Esq., F.S.A.
	21st July.	Meeting at Lingfield, Surrey, under R. GARRAWAY RICE, Esq., F.S.A.
	29th Sept.	Visit to the Churches of St. Margaret and St. John, Westminster.
1895.	12th Feb.	Tenth General Meeting in the hall of Colfe's Grammar School. — Paper by JOSEPH W. BROOKES, Esq., on the Influence of the Crusades on English Architecture (printed herewith).
	25th May.	Meeting at Chelsfield.—Paper on the Parish Church by LELAND L. DUNCAN, Esq., F.S.A. (subsequently printed in the Chelsfield Parish Magazine); Shoreham Church was visited later in the afternoon.
	22nd June.	Meeting at Ightham Mote, by permission of T. C. COLYER-FERGUSSON, Esq.
	20th July.	Meeting at Town Malling, and Papers on the Abbey and Parish Church by LELAND L. DUNCAN, Esq., F.S.A.
1896.	2nd May.	Meeting at Otford, under the Rev. Dr. HUNT, Rector, and visits to the Parish Church, the Manor House of the Archbishops of Canterbury, and the Well of St. Thomas.

1896. 6th June. Meeting at Cliffe-at-Hoo. The Rectory and Parish Church were visited, and subsequently Cooling Castle and Parish Church.

15th Aug. Meeting at Swanscombe, under the direction of H. STOPES, Esq., who also exhibited a portion of his collection of stone implements.

21st Dec. Meeting at St. Mary's National Schools.—Exhibitions by C. A. BRADFORD, Esq., P. W. AMES, Esq., F.S.A. (President), and R. GARRAWAY RICE, Esq., F.S.A.—Paper by LELAND L. DUNCAN, Esq., F.S.A., on an Inventory of the Contents of a Lewisham Husbandman's House in 1530.

1897. 24th Feb. Meeting in the hall of Colfe's Grammar School.—Paper by E. LEWIS, Esq., on the Cathedral and Abbey Churches of England, illustrated by lantern slides under the direction of W. HOWARD, Esq.

17th Mar. Twelfth General Meeting, in the Lewisham Parish Hall, Ladywell, and Address by H. STOPES, Esq., entitled "Pre-historic Antiquities in Kent."

Rules of the Society.

1. The objects of the Society are to study, and, as far as practicable, to record Antiquities, with special regard to the Parish of Lewisham.

2. The Society shall have for Officers: a President, Vice-Presidents, twelve Members of the Council, Honorary Secretary, and Honorary Treasurer, elected at the Annual Meeting in each year. The President, Vice-Presidents, Hon. Secretary, Hon. Treasurer, and nine Members of the Council shall be eligible for re-election.

3. Members shall be elected by the Council.

4. The Annual Subscription shall be 2s. 6d., payable on the 1st January. A Member may commute the 2s. 6d. for life by payment of two guineas.

5. The Annual Meeting shall be held in January.

6. Rules may be altered or rescinded, and Members excluded, at General Meetings called for the purpose by the Council.

List of Members.

David William Ames, Esq., 180 Adelaide Road, Brockley
Percy W. Ames, Esq., F.S.A., F.R.G.S., Lewisham Park
Mrs. P. W. Ames, Lewisham Park
Henry Edward Armstrong, Esq., F.R.S., PH.D., 55 Granville Park, Lewisham
F. T. Arnold, Esq., 82 London Street, Greenwich
Reuben Archer, Esq., Umberslade, Rushey Green, Catford
William Paley Baildon, Esq., F.S.A., 5 Stone Buildings, Lincoln's Inn, W.C.
James Stoddart Bain, Esq., 67 Mount Pleasant Road, Lewisham
William Edmund Ball, Esq., LL.D., 20 Dartmouth Row, Blackheath Hill
Arthur Oswald Barron, Esq., 6 Bramfield Road, Wandsworth Common
William Betts, Esq., 26 Limes Grove, Lewisham
Rev. Samuel Bickersteth, M.A., The Vicarage, Lewisham
Edward W. Brabrook, Esq., F.S.A., V.P.A.I., 178 Bedford Hill, Balham
Henry R. Brabrook, Esq., 178 Bedford Hill, Balham
Miss E. M. Brabrook, 178 Bedford Hill, Balham
Charles Angel Bradford, Esq., 21 Thornford Road, Lewisham
Canon R. Rhodes Bristow, M.A., St. Olave's, Eliot Park, Lewisham
Joseph W. Brookes, Esq., Pembroke Lodge, Slaithwaite Road, Lewisham
William Wallace Brown, Esq., 63 Cranfield Road, Brockley
Miss E. A. Langridge-Brown, 16 Belmont Park, Lee
C. S. Buck, Esq., 60 Queen Victoria Street, E.C.
C. E. Burrows, Esq., The Grange, Tottenham
J. M. Byrne, Esq., Bracklyn, Catford, S.E.
John Carline, Esq., C.E., Merivale, Catford Hill
Alfred Carroll, Esq., 68 Jerningham Road, New Cross
Walter Cooke, Esq., 30 Ashburnham Grove, Greenwich
Mrs. Emma Cooper, 12 Colville Gardens, Bayswater, W.
William F. Comber, Esq., 15 Lewisham Hill
T. W. Dannatt, Esq., 19 The Circus, Greenwich
Edward C. Davies, Esq., 173 Hither Green Lane, Lewisham
E. Emrys Davies, Esq., Sudgrove, Tyrwhitt Road, St. John's
Henry T. Davis, Esq., 115 Lewisham Road, S.E.
Charles W. Dawson, Esq., Tarbert, Lewisham Park
Mrs. C. W. Dawson, Tarbert, Lewisham Park
Walter Henry Dawson, Esq., Southend, Catford, S.E.
Frederick C. Deverell, Esq., Custom House, E.C.
Foster Dewick, Esq., 59 Clarendon Road, Lewisham
Joseph Dewick, Esq., 59 Clarendon Road, Lewisham

Rev. WILLIAM DODGE, B.A., 37 Trinity Square, Boro', S.E.
LELAND LEWIS DUNCAN, Esq., F.S.A., Rosslair, Lingards Road, Lewisham
WALTER M. EDGLEY, Esq., Pantin Lodge, 1 Chelsam Road, Clapham, W.
EDWIN H. EDINGER, Esq., 2 Lawn Terrace, Wisteria Road, Lewisham
Mrs. E. H. EDINGER, 2 Lawn Terrace, Wisteria Road, Lewisham
JOHN EMMERSON, Esq., 55 Court Hill Road, Lewisham
Sir J. FARNABY LENNARD, Bart., J.P., F.S.A., Wickham Court
F. FOUNTAIN, Esq., 44 Crooms Hill, Greenwich
ARNOLD FRANCKE, Esq., Fairlight, Lewisham Park
Mrs. GALZINI, 48 Limes Grove, Lewisham
SILVESTRO E. GALZINI, Esq., 8 Beechfield Road, Catford
Miss GANZ, 6 Belgrave Villas, Lee
Miss ALICE MARY GARDNER, 6 Ringstead Road, Catford
GEORGE E. GARDNER, Esq., 6 Ringstead Road, Catford
PERCY A. GLASSCOCK, Esq., 4 Belmont Hill, Lee
Mrs. P. A. GLASSCOCK, 4 Belmont Hill, Lee
Mrs. GOODBAN, 16 Belmont Park, Lee
ALBERT L. GUY, Esq., A.R.I.B.A., Rostrevor, Lewisham Park
Mrs. GUY, Rostrevor, Lewisham Park
GEORGE HAGGER, Esq., 38 George Lane, Lewisham
Mrs. HAGGER, 38 George Lane, Lewisham
Colonel W. HANDYSIDE, R.A., 45 Limes Grove, Lewisham
ALFRED L. HARDY, Esq., 40 Tyrwhitt Road, St. Johns
EDWARD L. C. P. HARDY, Esq., F.S.A., Bloomfield House, Bromley Road, Catford
J. HICKMAN, Esq., 378 Stanstead Road, Catford
Mrs. J. HICKMAN, 378 Stanstead Road, Catford
WILLIAM McC. HILL, Esq., Hyde Villa, Conduit Vale, Greenwich
WILLIAM HODGETTS, Esq., The Bank House, Lewisham
Mrs. HODGETTS, The Bank House, Lewisham
Miss ETHEL HODGETTS, The Bank House, Lewisham
THOMAS VINCENT HOLMES, Esq., F.G.S., 28 Crooms Hill, Greenwich
R. HOVENDEN, Esq., F.S.A., Heathcote, Park Hill Road, Croydon, Surrey
HARRY W. HOWARD, Esq., Maitland House, Greenwich
WALTER HOWGRAVE, Esq., A.C.A.
HERBERT JONES, Esq., F.S.A., 15 Montpelier Row, Blackheath
Rev. J. MORLAIS JONES, Hafod, Clarendon Road, Lewisham
ALFRED P. PERCIVAL KEEP, Esq., 26 Vanbrugh Park, Blackheath
DAVID KENNARD, Esq., Somerton, Bromley Road, Catford
ARTHUR KENNEDY, Esq., 69 Tyrwhitt Road, St. Johns
SAMUEL WAYLAND KERSHAW, Esq., F.S.A., M.A., Lambeth Palace, S.W.
HERBERT C. KIRBY, Esq., Linden Villa, Lewisham Park, S.E.
Mrs. KIRBY, Linden Villa, Lewisham Park, S.E.

Rev. BROOKE LAMBERT, B.C.L., M.A., The Vicarage, Greenwich
R. A. DOUGLAS LITHGOW, Esq., LL.D., M.D., F.S.A., V.P.R.S.L., 27a Lowndes Square, Belgrave Square, S.W.
H. LE JEUNE, Esq., 3 West Grove Terrace, Point Hill, Greenwich
E. LEWIS, Esq., 20 Wellington Road, Old Charlton
The LORD BISHOP OF LICHFIELD, The Palace, Lichfield
Rev. W. HOOK LONGSDON, M.A., 1 Merrick Square, Boro', S.E.
Sir JOHN LUBBOCK, Bart., M.P., F.R.S., High Elms, Farnboro', Kent
F. W. LUCAS, Esq., M.A., B.SC., Ferndale, Westcombe Park Road, Blackheath
BENJAMIN MARTEL, Esq., 7 Tressillian Crescent, St. Johns
Miss MARTEN, 78 Vanbrugh Park, Blackheath
Sir S. M. MARYON-WILSON, Bart., Charlton House, Charlton
JOHN J. MATTHIAS, Esq., High Street, Lewisham
WILLIAM JOHN MERCER, Esq., 12 Marine Terrace, Margate
HENRY GRAVE MORRIS, Esq., 269 Lewisham High Road, St. Johns
CHARLES MOTE, Esq., Myrtle Villa, 6 Slaithwaite Road, Lewisham
Mrs. C. MOTE, Myrtle Villa, 6 Slaithwaite Road, Lewisham
FRED. MOTE, Esq., M.A., LL.B., 9 Lansdown Road, Lee
Right Hon. The Earl of NORTHBROOK, 4 Hamilton Place, Piccadilly, W.
G. D. S. OLIVANT, Esq., F.R.S L., Summerfield, St. John's Road, Sidcup, Kent
Mrs. OLIVANT, Summerfield, St. John's Road, Sidcup, Kent
EDWARD H. OXENHAM, Esq., F.R.S.L., Keston Villa, Catford
Miss KATE PAKEMAN, Clyde Villa, Farley Road, Catford
Miss CARRY PAPWORTH, 47 Wisteria Road, Lewisham
Miss IDA PAPWORTH, 47 Wisteria Road, Lewisham
WILLIAM C. C. PARK, Esq., Beacon Lodge, Hither Green, Lewisham
Miss ALICE PARNABY
J. H. PORTER, Esq., 288 New Cross Road
Mrs. PORTER, 288 New Cross Road
CHARLES POWELL, Esq., 70 Brockley Road, New Cross
ERNEST VAN PUTTEN, Esq , Zion House, High Street, Lewisham
JOHN WALTER RAMSEY, Esq., 13 Northbrook Road, Lee
HERBERT J. REID, Esq., F.S.A., F.R.S.L., 11 St. James's Terrace, North Gate Regent's Park, N.W.
R. GARRAWAY RICE, Esq., F.S.A., Carpenter's Hill, Pulboro', Sussex
Mrs. R. GARRAWAY RICE, 23 Cyril Mansions, Prince of Wales Road, S.W.
HENRY SAMUEL RICHARDSON, Esq., 163 Algernon Road, Lewisham
WALTER ROBINS, Esq., B.SC., 9 Northbrook Road, Lee
Rev. EDWARD CECIL ROBINSON, M.A., Hanbury, Burton-on-Trent
GEORGE ROBINSON, Esq., 17 Gloucester Place, Greenwich
Mrs. ROBINSON, 17 Gloucester Place, Greenwich
FREDERICK GEORGE RÜCKER, Esq., 4 Vanbrugh Terrace, Blackheath

Miss RÜCKER, 4 Vanbrugh Terrace, Blackheath
ROBERT W. RUDD, Glanville, 13 Kings Hall Road, New Beckenham
Mrs. R. W. RUDD, Glanville, 13 Kings Hall Road, New Beckenham
WILLIAM RUSHTON, Esq., M.R.C.S., 32 Harley Street, W.
Miss SABINE, 21 Thornford Road, Lewisham
JAMES EBENEZER SAUNDERS, Esq., J.P., F.S.A., F.G.S., F.L.S., Chelvistone, Eltham Road, Lee
MARTIN L. SAUNDERS, Esq., F.R.I.B.A., 20 Southbrook Road, Lee
JOHN F. SHERRIS, Esq., 1 George Lane, Lewisham
Mrs. SHOVE, High Street, Lewisham
Miss SIMES, 103 Belvedere Road, Upper Norwood
DAVID CHISHOLM SIMPSON, Esq., 199 Camberwell Grove, Denmark Hill
EUGENE SIMON, Esq., 104 Greenwich Road
EDWARD C. SINKLER, Esq., 55 Clarendon Road, Lewisham
CURWEN SISTERSON, Esq., F.R.S.L., Bognor, Sussex
SCOTT SISTERSON, Esq., 53 Devonshire Road, Greenwich
WALTER SLATER, Esq., 174 High Street, Lewisham
J. E. SMITH, Esq., Town Hall, Westminster
JAMES SPENCER, Esq., 121 Lewisham Road, S.E.
JOHN M. STONE, Esq., M.A., 29 Lee Park, Blackheath
JOHN W. STONE, Esq., Plas Isa, 126 Breakspear Road, St. Johns
EDWIN HENRY STRAW, Esq., The Woodlands, Rushey Green, Catford
EDWARD STYLES, Esq., 20 Vesta Road, Brockley
Rev. GEORGE B. TATUM, M.A., St. Saviour's Presbytery, 157 High Street, Lewisham
T. H. TERRY, Esq., 63 Perry Hill, Catford
ERNEST THOMPSON, Esq., Ivedale, Queen's Road, Clock House, Beckenham
ARTHUR T. TODD WHITE, Esq.
Mrs. HERBERT TRENDELL, 14 Ladbroke Square, Notting Hill, W.
JOHN JAMES TROTT, Esq., Romford, Essex
Miss AMY WALLIS, Terrace House, 153 Old Kent Road, S.E.
Rev. J. BENSON WALSHE, M.A., The Vicarage, St. Ann's, Bermondsey, S.E.
CHARLES WELCH, Esq., F.S.A., Guildhall Library
L. J. DE WHALLEY, Esq., B.SC., M.P.S., M.S.C.I., F.C.S., 26 Park Place, Greenwich
THOMAS WHITE, Esq., 133 High Street, Lewisham
WILLIAM WHITMORE, Esq., 20 Vanbrugh Park, Blackheath
Mrs. W. WHITMORE, 20 Vanbrugh Park, Blackheath
EDWIN ANDREW WINDER, Esq., Stanmore Villa, Hither Green, Lewisham
Mrs. E. A. WINDER, Stanmore Villa, Hither Green, Lewisham
EDMUND HIGHAM WRIGHT, Esq., Woodhall Villa, Adelaide Road, Brockley
Rev. G. MALLOWS YOUNGMAN, M.A., 24 King William Street, Greenwich,

Publications of the Society.

The Registers of St. Margaret's, Lee, 1579=1754, with extracts from Wills and full Indices of Persons and Places. Edited by LELAND L. DUNCAN and ARTHUR O. BARRON. Imperial Octavo, cloth, 8s. post free.

The Monumental Inscriptions in the Church and Churchyard of St. Mary, Lewisham, with Indices of Persons and Places. Edited by HERBERT C. KIRBY and LELAND L. DUNCAN. Imperial Octavo, cloth, 8s. post free.

A Calendar of all the Wills relating to the County of Kent, proved in the Prerogative Court of Canterbury, 1384-1559, arranged lexicographically, and with Index of Places. Edited by LELAND L. DUNCAN, F.S.A. Imperial Octavo, cloth, interleaved with stout writing paper, 10s. 6d. post free.

The Parish Registers of St. Mary, Lewisham, 1558=1750, being such portions as were saved from the fire of 1830, with numerous extracts from Wills of Persons formerly residing at Lewisham, and full Indices of Persons and Places. Edited by LELAND L. DUNCAN, F.S.A. Imperial Octavo, cloth, One Guinea post free.

De Luci the Loyal, Founder of Lessness Abbey, by W. E. BALL, LL.D. Octavo, cloth, One Shilling.

The Parish Church of St. Mary, Lewisham: its Building and Re-building, with some account of the Vicars of Lewisham, by LELAND L. DUNCAN, F.S.A. Cloth, Illustrated, 3s. 6d.; 4s. post free.

The Registers of Orpington, Kent, 1560=1754, with extracts from Wills and full Indices of Persons and Places. Edited by HERBERT C. KIRBY. Imperial Octavo, cloth, One Guinea, post free.

The Headmasters of Colfe's Grammar School, Lewisham Hill, 1652=1894, by LELAND L. DUNCAN. F.S.A. Octavo, paper, 6d.; cloth, 1s. 6d.

The Life and Times of Abraham Colfe, Vicar of Lewisham and Founder of the Grammar School, by the Rev. THOMAS BRAMLEY, D.D. Small Octavo, paper, 2s. [Only a few copies remain.]

On the Derivation and Meaning of the name "Lewisham," by the Rev. Professor W. W. SKEAT. Octavo, paper, 1d.

The Influence of the Crusades on Architecture in England, by JOSEPH W. BROOKES. Octavo, cloth, 1s.

Applications for copies of the above Publications should be made to the Society's Printer:

Charles North, Blackheath Printing Works, S.E.

Lewisham Antiquarian Society.

On the Derivation and Meaning of the name "Lewisham,"

by

W. W. Skeat.

On the Influence of the Crusades upon English Architecture,

by

Joseph W. Brookes.

1897.

On the Derivation and Meaning of the name Lewisham.

In Hasted's History of Kent the name Lewisham is stated " to be derived from *Les* or Leswes [læswe, læsu] in Saxon, " signifying pastures, and *ham*, a town or village," and this statement has been very generally copied by local writers.

An examination of early charters in which Lewisham is mentioned clearly shows the above view to be a mistaken one, and Professor Skeat has kindly favoured the Society with an authoritative pronouncement on the question.

The form of the name varies as follows:—

Liofshema	{	Charter of Aethelberht of Wessex, A.D. 862. Kemble's Charters, No. 287.
Lieuesham	{	Charter of Ethelswitha, daughter of Alfred the Great, A.D. 918.*
Leofsuhaema	{	Charter of Aethebred, 987. Kemble's Charters, No. 657.
Liefesham	{	Vow of Edward the Confessor, A.D. 1006.*
Leuesham	{	Charter of Edward, A.D. 1044. Kemble's Charters, No. 771.
Levesham	-	Doomsday Book, A.D. 1086.
Liefesham	-	Charter of William Rufus.*
Leuesham	-	temp. Edward III, 1370.*
Lewsham	-	16th and 17th centuries.†
Lewisham	-	present day.

Professor Skeat writes:—

The A.S. *læsu*, a pasture, became *leese* in Elizabethan English. It is now spelt *lees, leas, lease* and *leys*. The last spelling suggests that it is a plural, which is not the case. The word *lea*, A.S. *leāh*, a fallow-field, is a totally different word, with a mere accidental resemblance of sound. It is also spelt *ley, lay, leigh*, and is common in place-names.

The A.S. *læswe* is the dative case of the form *læsu* above.

---

* Vide " Hasted's History of Kent " (*Ed.* Drake).
† Parish Registers and other Documents.

Nevertheless, it produced the form *leasowe* or *leasow*, pronounced *lesser* in Shropshire.

The A.S. *lǣsu* would have given us *Leesham*, which is not right. The A.S. *lǣswe* would have given us *Leasow-ham*; the contracted form of which would have been *Lesham*, pronounced *Lesham* or *Lessum*. This, likewise, is not right. It shows that all that Hasted (or those upon whom he relied) did was to guess freely without testing the results.

The quotations given above furnish the right clue as to the derivation of the name, but they require a little explanation.

In the forms Liofshema and Leofsuhaema, the –*a* is only a case-ending. The phrase "Lēofsuhǣma mearc," as it is found in charters, means "the mark or boundary of the inhabitants of Lēofsuhām"; haēma being the genitive plural of haēme, a nominative plural signifying "men belonging to a *hām* or farmstead."

Liof is the Kentish spelling of A.S. *lēof*. *Lēof* is the modern English *lief*, which was once an adjective and meant "dear." In *Liofs-hēma*, the *s* cannot be a genitive suffix, as that was –*es*, but it is the first letter of a second syllable; it stands for *Līof-s'*.

In *Lēof-su* the second syllable is also incomplete; it stands for *Lēofsu'*.

The middle portion of a name is often partially suppressed, as in Lem'ster for Leominster, and the like. *Leof-su'* obviously stands for *Lēof-suna*, the genitive case of *Lēof-sunu*, which was a fairly common name, occurs in Kentish and Southern Charters, and simply means "dear son."

Thus the obvious sense is "Lēof-sunu's home," or a farmstead in which lived a man named Lēof-sunu (lit. dear son).

As for the pronounciation, the modern English Leveson, which is the modern English form of Leof-sunu, is pronounced Lewson. So in modern English, Lewisham means Leveson's-home; or, remembering that the genitive case of *sunu* (son) did *not* end in –*s*, but in –*a* (which now-a-days would disappear) it would more exactly be represented by "Lewson-home," and this by contraction regularly becomes *Lews-ham* or even *Lusam*, as it was phonetically spelt in the seventeenth century.

Then popular etymology substituted the known name *Lewis*, for the form *Lus*, which had lost all meaning, and the –*is* of Lewis being now generally plainly heard, the form *Lewis-ham* has become fixed.

It is necessary to add that some exception was taken to this etymology in Notes and Queries, 8 S. xi. 311; but the writer of the note has since kindly informed me that he wholly withdraws his objection, and that my solution is certainly correct.

W. W. SKEAT.

On the Influence of the Crusades upon English Architecture.

It is indisputable that the Crusades exercised an enormous influence upon the nations of Western Europe, and amongst them upon our own country; in many ways the Holy Wars led to an immense development of individual freedom, of commerce, of science and art, and of intellectual activity generally. "Conflict," it has been well said, "seems to be necessary for the development of the finer attributes of the human mind"; or as Sir G. Gilbert Scott wrote, with a somewhat narrower application of the same idea: "Though war and bloodshed are in them-
" selves hostile to art, there can be no doubt that the excitement
" of the human mind resulting from great national struggles
" has tended to produce great advances in art . . . . The
" period of the Crusades was one of deep-seated mental excite-
" ment; youthful energy pervaded every branch of art; every-
" thing seemed to experience a new, a generous and vigorous
" impulse."

The various peoples who took part in the Crusades were brought into contact with each other to a degree for which before there had never been opportunity, and the natural and inevitable result of this intercourse was a mutually beneficial interchange of thought. Moreover men brought back from the East—for centuries the nursery of art, learning and civilization whilst the West was shrouded in the darkness of barbarism—new ideas on many subjects, which had a powerful effect in shaping the destinies of the Western nations. Architecture could not fail to partcipate in the great general awakening thus produced, and my present object is to show as far as I can in what manner and to what extent that art was so influenced in this country. The influence was of two distinct kinds: (1) a general impulse resulting from the great awakening and mental excitement above referred to, and (2) the effect of actual practical ideas imported from the East by survivors returning from the Crusades. Of these it is difficult to decide which had the greater result.

In the consideration of the first named division of the subject it does not appear advisable or even possible to separate England from the other nations of Western Europe. Undoubtedly France was more profoundly affected by the Crusades than was this country, during the earlier portion of the period over which the conflict extended, both because she took a far more prominent part than England in the first two Crusades, and also, in less degree, by reason of her comparative nearness to the seat of the struggle; hence some portion of the influence upon our architecture came to us through the medium of France, as will be seen hereafter. Still, the great movement affected all the Western nations in the same way, and produced in them similar results, although in varying degrees. As already stated, increased activity and inventiveness in the arts were among the effects produced, and it is reasonable to suppose that the influence upon architecture would be especially profound, because the Crusades were at once the result and the cause of deep religious feeling, whilst the noblest monuments of architectural skill have ever been those erected for religious purposes. Much was done in the name of the Crusades which reflects the greatest discredit upon the Christianity of the time, and many were the motives that led men to flock to the East; nevertheless it cannot be denied that religious feeling was the main cause. As the movement increased, its own vehemence added fresh fuel to the flames; the religious enthusiasm spread from one to another until all were infected by it—those who perforce remained at home as well as those who took active part in the struggle. It was natural that some of this religious excitement should find vent in the building and adornment of churches, and we may fairly assume that the clergy of that day would not be backward in urging upon their flocks the duty of contributing liberally towards so good a cause, especially those persons who were themselves unable or unwilling to become Crusaders.

Despite the plunder obtained in the East there is little doubt that most of those who returned in safety from the Crusades did so in an impoverished condition. Evidence is not lacking upon this point. Such folk would come back possessed of new tastes and ideas, but often without the means of carrying them into effect. On the other hand, those who had remained peaceably at home adding to their wealth—it may be at the expense of their more enthusiastic and adventurous countrymen—possessed the means but not the new ideas; and these conditions necessarily tended to give predominance to the general or *indirect* stimulus with regard to the development of architecture, rather than to the practical or direct influence. It must not be forgotten that many monks and other ecclesiastics, themselves often the chief architects and builders of the time, accompanied the Crusaders, and were in some cases the agents in the introduction of Eastern novelties; still, the conditions above set forth must have exerted an important effect in limiting and determining the course of development of Western architecture.

Passing now to the second division of my subject, the influence of the actual concrete ideas brought over by Crusaders, it is advisable first to clear the ground by describing briefly the condition of architecture in this country about the date of the first Crusade. The general *form* of the churches was already fixed, the basilica plan upon which it was founded having long been modified into practically the same as that invariably used during the succeeding five or six centuries. To the original rectangular basilica-church the transept had been added, giving the whole building the form of the Latin cross, and the original length of the eastern arm had been increased to afford accommodation for the priests or monks taking part in the services. The basilican apse was generally retained at the eastern extremity, but square terminations were by no means uncommon in this country in pre-Norman churches; a central tower at the intersection of the arms, known as the *crossing*, was also a frequent feature. As examples I may name the Saxon church on the castle hill at Dover—which has a square east-end and a central tower; and that at Worth in Sussex—with its eastern apse; each possessing a short transept. The larger churches erected during the latter half of the eleventh century (in the Norman branch of the Romanesque style) had generally a *nave* with *side aisles*, the latter separated from the former by the great arcades supporting the superstructure; and over the vaulted ceilings of the aisles were galleries (*triforia*) opening into the nave by another tier of arches, whilst above these again were the *clerestory* windows. Obviously, then, the general plan and arrangement of our churches had already been developed, and it is to matters of detail that we must look in order to find evidence, if any exist, of the influence of the Crusades.

The details of Norman work before the first Crusade, shortly summarised, were as follows:—The whole style was essentially heavy and massive; the great arcades were supported upon square or rectangular piers, or circular—sometimes octagonal—columns of great diameter, with capitals generally of the "cushion" shape, occasionally having simple volutes at the angles. The arches were semi-circular, with square edges or plain roll mouldings, and perhaps sparingly decorated with the zig-zag, hatched, or billet ornaments; windows and doors semi-circular-headed and undivided. Some of these characteristics had been derived from the East (*e.g.* the "cushion" capital), but their origin does not concern our present object, which is to separate, as far as possible, from the total effect of Eastern influence that particular portion of it which is attributable to the Crusades.

Perhaps the most important point that can arise in connection with this subject, is that of the origin and introduction of the *pointed arch*. It is unnecessary to dwell here upon the enormous effect on Western architecture generally which resulted from the adoption of this feature; it is indeed the very essence of the perfected Gothic style, the full development of which without it would have been impossible. According to one widely accepted theory of its origin, the pointed arch was suggested by the intersecting arcades of semi-circular arches common in Norman buildings; this, however, seems highly improbable in face of the fact that the pointed arch had been in common use in the East long centuries before it was employed by Western Europeans, and also for other reasons which will appear later. The actual date of the earliest architectural use of this feature is unknown, but it is sufficient to point out that it occurs in Saracen buildings of the eighth, ninth and tenth centuries in Egypt, and to name the Mosque of Ibn-Touloun at Cairo (finished about A.D. 879) as an excellent example of its use.

The writers of the article on Architecture in the *Encyclopædia Britannica* (9th edition) assert that no European nation can claim any decided priority in the use of the pointed arch, but that it was introduced by the principal Western nations—sparingly at first—practically at the same time; that is, in the interval between the first and second Crusades. It is true that arches of pointed form were employed in certain churches in Aquitaine and Anjou (*e.g.*, St. Front Perigueux, Souillac, Fontevrault) at an earlier date; but the custom was entirely a local one, and passed out of use without extending even to the more northerly provinces of France itself. At Fontevrault pointed arches support Norman round-arch work of a later date,* showing that the former were abandoned even in the provinces named; these exceptional instances may therefore be safely neglected in the present enquiry. An early example of pointed arches constructed by Europeans is that of the Church of the Holy Sepulchre at Jerusalem, which was in great part re-built by the Crusaders during the first few years of the twelfth century, the pointed arches occurring in their portion of the work. It is surely a significant fact that this early instance occurs *in the East*, and in conjunction with other features undoubtedly inspired by Eastern models. Sir Gilbert Scott considered that the pointed arch must have been known to the Western nations before the end of the eleventh century, but that those nations were specially reminded of it by the Crusades.† Amongst early examples of

---

* Fergusson's *History of Architecture*.

† Since writing this paper I find Professor Freeman in his *History of the Norman Conquest* says:—"The use of the pointed arch as the main "constructive feature was, there can hardly be a doubt, brought back "to Western Europe by the Crusaders."

the use of this form in England are the following :—The Round Church at Northampton, built by one Simon de St. Liz—*a Crusader*—who died in 1127; Malmesbury Abbey (1115-1139); Fountains (1132-1140); Kirkstall (1152-1180); the work in these churches being otherwise purely Norman in character, at all events in those portions of each where the early pointed arches occur.

For present purposes, therefore, I assume that one of the results of the Crusades was the introduction of the pointed arch into this country, although it may be necessary later to qualify this and other conclusions at which I provisionally arrive.

The Eastern nations, although the first to use the pointed arch, did not fully recognise its capabilities, nor develop a system of true *pointed architecture;* that was reserved for the peoples of Western Europe—for France, England and Germany. These nations first employed this form of arch for its greater stability and decreased thrust as compared with the round arch, the latter being retained some time longer for decorative purposes. Authorities (Fergusson, Scott and others) agree that the pointed arch was always first introduced for wide spans of vaulting, or the support of towers and gables; in wide arches of main arcades; and not until it became customary in those and similar positions for practical reasons was it employed for purposes of ornament and taste. If this view—that the pointed arch was first employed here for constructive reasons—be strictly accurate, it surely goes far to dispose of the argument already referred to that the form was derived from, or suggested by, the arcades of intersecting semi-circular arches so often found in Norman buildings, but which are, of course, *purely decorative*, serving no structural use whatever. I am inclined to think, too, that true pointed arches were used quite as early as the interlaced variety of ornamental arcading.

The suggestion of the pointed arch was probably first obtained from buildings of Arab origin, but most of the remaining traces of Eastern influence upon our architecture indicate their derivation from Byzantine sources. This is, of course, just what might be expected, the Byzantine style having, by the end of the eleventh century, been so long prevalent in the countries which came under the observation of the Crusaders. Not only had it spread throughout the formerly vast area of the Eastern Roman Empire, including Asia Minor and Syria, where numerous remains of buildings in the style still exist; but many of its features had been borrowed by the Arabs and combined with additions of their own to form the *Saracenic* style.

Byzantine architecture was founded upon that of Rome, with modifications derived from Greek models; and its sacred buildings were based upon two forms—the round-domed church and the rectangular basilica church. By the time of Justinian (sixth century) the cruciform shape was developed by the addition of true transepts, generally roofed with a dome at the crossing, the arms also frequently being covered in the same manner. Ornament was profusely introduced into the interiors, based, as a rule, upon Greek classic forms, but altered in detail. Columns, bases, capitals and friezes were covered with ornament, Greek in conception, which, as time went on, became increasingly inferior in artistic excellence—cold, stiff and shallow. Many capitals especially were of Greek character, their designs founded upon the Corinthian order, both in general shape and decoration, but with the foliage flattened upon the bell, the projecting volutes having a stiff and formal effect. Another style of classic foliage was often employed, either in connection with or apart from the Corinthianesque type, consisting of plain smooth leaves, curled over at the tips, with straight unserrated edges—a form originally derived from Egpyt, like many more of the details employed by the Greeks. Other forms of foliar ornament adopted from various sources were modified into peculiarly characteristic Byzantine varieties, which are unmistakable wherever met with. The Crusaders necessarily came in contact with many noble specimens of true classic Greek architecture, as well as the somewhat debased forms used by the Byzantines. The churches of the latter were richly decorated with mosaics, a style of art more extensively adopted in Italy and France than in England, where remains thereof are comparatively rare. Other features of Byzantine architecture will be touched upon later as their effect upon our own buildings is considered.

Next, perhaps, in importance to the influence of the pointed arch as regards permanent effect upon our architecture, was that exercised by the classic and pseudo-classic foliage just referred to, and by other kinds of similar ornamental detail. During the latter half of the twelfth century, as the pure Norman style in this country developed into the Transitional, the carving of the capitals and other decorative features, hitherto rude in character, gradually became more elaborate and artistic in treatment. The most notable instances are those in which foliage of distinctly Greek or Byzantine type is employed, the best known examples being the capitals in the choir and retro-choir of Canterbury Cathedral, worked under the direction of William of Sens and his pupil and successor William the Englishman, between 1175 and 1184. Some of these are of great artistic beauty, and although the source of their inspiration is unmistakable, the designs vary from those of the type upon which they are founded; moreover, the capitals differ from one another, instead of being mere reproductions of one pattern as in classical

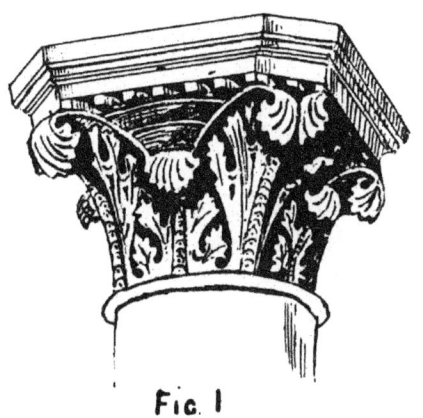

Fig. 1

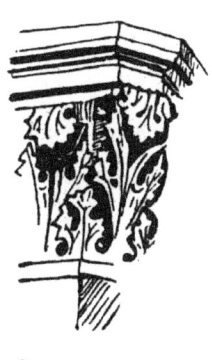

Fig. 2

Fig. 3

Fig. 4

buildings. One very important feature is the substitution for the volutes at the angles of Corinthian capitals, of curled bunches of conventional foliage, some of which are distinctly of classic or Byzantine character, whilst others differ from the acanthus type, although obviously derived therefrom. Of the first kind figs. 1 and 2 are examples, both from the work of William of Sens; and of the second, figs. 3 and 4 dating from the time of his successor, the English William. Numerous instances of capitals with foliage of Byzantine character occur elsewhere in this country. Two remarkable examples are figured in Sir Gilbert Scott's *Lectures on Mediæval Architecture*, one from St. Cross at Winchester, the other from Bridlington Priory; in both the form of the leaves employed is characteristically Byzantine, and of a type very common in Eastern churches, *e.g.*, SS. Sergius and Bacchus at Constantinople. Very similar capitals occur in England at Lincoln Cathedral, in the north-west portal; at the Temple Church, London, and elsewhere. In the aforesaid doorway at Lincoln the ordinary stiff acanthus leaf is employed together with the more distinctive Byzantine forms; moreover, two adjoining shaft capitals show, in one, small classic volutes at the angles, and in the other, Byzantine foliage in their place, as at Canterbury. Ruder specimens of Byzantinesque ornament are very freely scattered all over England upon capitals, fonts, tympana of doorways, &c. of twelfth century date, and some allusion will be made to them below.

The influence exercised by this new decorative work was important in its results. The peculiar curled foliage first introduced at the angles of capitals in place of the classic volutes, became developed into—or at least formed a principal factor in the development of—the so-called *stiff-leaved foliage* characteristic of thirteenth century (or early English) work; the ribs and stems of the acanthus leaves being gradually transformed into the stalks of the later foliage. Many examples might be named in proof of this assertion, and figures of four specimens are here given. Fig. 5 is from the south-east transept at Canterbury; figs. 6 and 7 are the lower portions of crockets from Bishop Bridport's Monument at Salisbury (c. 1246); and fig. 8 from Salisbury Chapter house. The capital from Canterbury shows the foliage still in a partially developed state, whilst 6 and 7 show it in a more perfect and advanced condition. These two specimens are especially valuable and interesting, presenting as they do straight acanthus-like foliage in actual conjunction with the new English "stiff-leaved" variety, thus clearly marking the transition from the one form to the other. In fig. 8 the acanthus is dropped altogether.

But the Corinthianesque foliage was not the only kind of

ornamental detail introduced from the East during Norman and Transitional times; other varieties of carved capitals and many moulding designs owed their origin to Eastern influence. Bridlington Priory, Wootton Church (Gloucestershire), St. Peter's (Northampton), Oxford Cathedral, the crypt at Canterbury, and scores of other buildings of similar date that might be named, afford capitals with carvings of unmistakably Byzantine character. In many of these, as in the portal at Lincoln above referred to, the "bead" ornament—employed in the classic styles and very freely also by the Byzantines—is profusely introduced. The details of the elaborate late Norman and Transition doorways of which we possess so many rich examples, are often of pronounced Byzantine type; those at Shobden in Herefordshire (c. 1141) and Kilpeck in the same county are cases in point. (Excellent reproductions of these portals are to be seen in the Crystal Palace.) Some of the shafts at Shobden are decorated with a close basket-work design—a form of ornament freely used by, although not peculiar to, the Byzantines; and the beaded strap-work also occurring at Shobden, as well as in numerous other localities, is highly characteristic of Byzantine art. An excellent example of Anglo-Byzantine moulding is the outer one over the Prior's doorway on the south side of the nave at Ely, which closely resembles one upon the Lincoln north-west portal. Scattered throughout the country, too, are numerous examples of figure subjects—zoological, mythological and biblical—carved upon shaft capitals, tympana of doorways, fonts and other situations, which are unmistakably of Byzantine inspiration. Many of these occur in the small churches of remote country districts; some are well finished like the relief over the Prior's door at Ely, others ludicrous in their grotesque rudeness.* At Fordington, Dorset, a sculptured group over the doorway represents the supposed miraculous incident at the seige of Antioch in 1098, when St. George came to the aid of the Crusaders and helped to defeat the Saracens. Certainly there is no doubt as to the Eastern source of that particular group, or the means of its introduction into England.

A common feature in the more important Byzantine churches was the employment of columns of ornamental marbles; these occur, for instance, in the church of St. Sophia at Constantinople and the Dome of the Rock at Jerusalem. The example in this respect had been set by older classical buildings; indeed, the remains of these were despoiled to obtain columns for the Byzantine churches. It is not improbable that the use

---

* Many specimens are figured in *Early Christian Symbolism in Great Britain and Ireland before the XIII Century*. By Mr. J. Romilly Allen, F.S.A. (Scot).

in this country of polished Purbeck marble and other ornamental varieties of stone for columns and shafts may have been suggested by the Eastern practice. The earliest instances of the use here of such materials are, so far as I know, those afforded by the round nave of the Templar's Church, London, and the choir of Canterbury, both consecrated in 1185. The fine groups of columns in the first-named building are of Purbeck marble—a very suggestive fact, the church having been designed upon the model of that of the Holy Sepulchre at Jerusalem, which, as I have already mentioned, was largely rebuilt by the Crusaders early in the twelfth century. The practice of grouping separate columns, two or more together, as in the churches just named (Canterbury and the Temple) and elsewhere, may have been adopted from the East, where it had previously been employed both in Byzantine and Arab architecture. After the date above mentioned, 1185 or thereabouts, the custom of employing ornamental marbles for columns and detached shafts, especially the latter, became increasingly common, and was one of the specially distinctive features of early thirteenth century work.

The employment of small shafts in recesses of large piers and jambs of windows, for supporting the sub-arches of triforia, the arch groups in clerestories, and other purposes structural and decorative, had arisen before the time of the Crusades; but it is highly probable the more frequent use of such shafts in the East, particularly in Arab architecture, caused them to be more freely introduced here. The Normans could only obtain the requisite strength in their buildings by massive construction, but the Arabs had acquired a better knowledge of the scientific use of materials, and were consequently able to erect structures remarkable for their grace and lightness. These qualities were characteristic of buildings of Arab origin, and the effect of the latter upon our own architecture was naturally in the same direction, assisting the enormous change in those respects which so strongly marked the development of the true Gothic from the Romanesque style. In this connection I may quote the following paragraph from a magazine article by Dean Spence, of Gloucester: "The monks became weary of the stern "plainness of Norman architecture; lighter and seemingly more "graceful forms of tracery and arch had been brought back by "successive bands of Crusaders from the East," which were gradually introduced. This passage accurately describes in general terms the influence of Saracenic architecture upon our own, but I am unable to understand the reference to *tracery*, if the term be used in its usual technical sense. There exists in this country such an unbroken series of examples showing the development of tracery from the simple piercing of the triforium tympana at Peterborough (c. 1140), or the similar window-head at St. Maurice's, York, now alas destroyed, to the elaborate fourteenth century windows and triforium openings as at Ely, and those of the Perpendicular style of which so many noble examples are preserved—that no room remains in the sequence for the introduction of Eastern patterns. The case is altogether different with the Corinthianesque capital, the pointed arch, the marble shaft, all of which were necessarily introduced in a complete form. The term *tracery* in the passage quoted, however, may possibly be used in a wider sense to include capital sculpture, for instance, and other similar details; it is, I believe, sometimes loosely applied in this manner.

Another decorative feature which became increasingly common in the thirteenth century was the trefoil arch. This form was, almost without doubt, imitated from Eastern work; indeed, arch foliation generally was probably suggested by oriental forms. The breaking up of the inner curves of arches into a number of pointed or rounded indentations, transforming the plain arch into one of trefoil, cinquefoil, or multifoil shape, is, and was many centuries ago, a striking characteristic of Arab architecture. The custom was introduced into England early in the twelfth century or in the last few years of the eleventh century.

It has frequently been suggested that many of the designs used in diaper wall-decoration, which came into use in the twelfth century, and afterwards more freely, were copied from or suggested by the patterns of woven or embroidered fabrics imported from the East, partly, no doubt, by the Crusaders. It is on record that Byzantine churches were often adorned with hangings of this nature, the patterns upon which were made up of repetitions of the same conventional floral or foliar design, enclosed within square or lozenge-shaped compartments. In Byzantine paintings, frescoes and mosaics, the robes of personages, walls of buildings and articles of furniture represented, are generally decorated with set patterns, similar in nature to those used in diaper work.

The capitals of pure Norman work in England are generally of the so-called cushion shape—convex; but in Transition work many are concave in the bell, especially those of Corinthianesque type. If the foliage be stripped off a capital of this description the body left bears a tolerably close resemblance to the bell of the plain thirteenth century capital so commonly used throughout the country. For a true Early English capital the round abacus is, of course, required; this, I believe, was first employed by William the Englishman in Canterbury crypt, but the germ of the idea seems to exist in some of the classically derived capitals

Fig. 5

Fig. 6

Fig. 7

Fig. 8

such as those at Canterbury (fig. 1 and 4), and others at Lincoln, Oxford and Oakham Castle, in all of which the true abacus rests upon a round moulding crowning the bell, and usually partly hidden by the foliage.

Amongst the various features I have referred to as having probably or possibly been introduced through the agency of the Crusades, some have been permanent in their influence (*e.g.*, the pointed arch, the Byzantinesque foliage, etc.), others were merely taken up as temporary fashions or were used in individual cases only. In the latter class I may mention one or two examples other than those already adduced. Thus at Holywell Church, Oxford (early twelfth century) there is an arch of the peculiar horse-shoe shape common in Arabic architecture. Arches of horse-shoe type occur also in Norman vaulting, as at Peterborough, but these come under a different category, having been used for structural reasons to obtain increased height where, later, pointed arches would have been employed; whilst the Holywell arch was obviously adopted for ornamental effect, as the structural requirements would have been far more efficiently served by a pointed arch. A more important influence is seen in the form of the round churches built in avowed imitation of the church of the Holy Sepulchre at Jerusalem; of these only five now remain, the Temple Church, London, Cambridge, Northampton, Little Maplestead and Ludlow. The first church erected by the Knights Templars in London was on the south side of what is now Holborn, and it is interesting to know that in the last century the removal of some old houses in Southampton Buildings laid bare the foundations of that earlier church, showing that it also was built upon the same circular plan. The date of the church was about the middle of the twelfth century, or perhaps a little earlier. The round church at Northampton, built by one Simon de St. Liz, a Crusader, contains pointed arches which, if part of the original work, form an early example of their use, seeing that St. Liz died in 1127. A peculiarity in plan of some Byzantine churches was the use of two transepts, and similar features of some of our cathedrals—Rochester, Lincoln, Salisbury and others—may have been suggested by those Eastern models.

Of the special features of English architecture, so briefly and imperfectly described above, some were *undoubtedly* due to, or influenced by, ideas introduced into this country during the Crusade period, whilst others were *probably* so influenced. It remains now for me to point out that we are not justified in attributing the whole of such influence to the Crusades.

In the first place, the Crusaders themselves were not the only men who visited the territories lying about the eastern end of the Mediterranean during the eleventh, twelfth and thirteenth centuries; pilgrims to Palestine were numerous long before the first crusade was organized—indeed, one of the strongest reasons urged to induce the Christians of western Europe to join the expedition was the fact that the pilgrims who, in the time of the Arab occupation, had been allowed to visit Jerusalem without molestation were, after the conquest of the Holy Land by the Turks in the middle of the eleventh century, subjected to gross ill-treatment and many indignities. The number of pilgrims so persecuted must have been large, otherwise the excitement and enthusiasm aroused would not have been so intense; and we know that in the eleventh century—after the passing away of the period of general stagnation, caused by the popular belief that the end of the world was to come in the year A.D. 1000—a multitude of pilgrims flocked to Jerusalem, including, amongst Englishmen, Sweyn, son of Earl Godwin, and Ealdred, Archbishop of York. Thus communication between this country and the Byzantine Empire, Asia Minor and the Holy Land was not established for the first time when the Crusaders passed through or invaded those territories in 1096-9. Again, commercial relations with the East, which existed prior to that date, must have led in some degree to an exchange of ideas as well as commodities.

Another channel for the spread of Eastern architectural forms was the existence of fraternities of masons, which, numbering in their ranks architects of Byzantine nationality, travelled from town to town in western Europe, as required, to aid in the erection of churches. But it is hardly likely that this influence reached England to any considerable extent, judging from the absence of any buildings undoubtedly Eastern in *plan*, other than those which are known to have been erected by the Crusaders.

Although opportunities thus existed before the closing years of the eleventh century, for the introduction of oriental ideas, the soil was not in fit state to receive the seed, which, therefore, could not spring up in full vigour; it was only after the rising of that great wave of religious enthusiasm—of which, as I have endeavoured to show, the Crusades were in a sense at once the result and the cause—that the nation afforded sufficient "depth of earth" for those seeds firmly to take root and bear fruit.

It must be admitted that England was for a long time slow to absorb the new ideas—slower than her nearest neighbours on the Continent; but for this backwardness there were special reasons. In the first Crusade England played but a small part, mainly for the reason that in 1095, less than thirty years after the Battle of Hastings, the country, although conquered, was not subdued; at all events the Norman nobles, as a rule, did not feel themselves sufficiently secure in their new possessions to risk a prolonged absence from home. Hence the influence of the Crusades during the greater part of the twelfth century came to us partially through the medium of France. Capitals of Corinthianesque character of the eastern type occur there earlier and more plentifully than in England; the earliest French examples (at St. Front Perigueux) probably date from before the first Crusade, and were copied, together with the general plan of the building, from the church of St. Mark at Venice, the work of Byzantine architects. A few other churches in the south of France possessing similar features date from about the same time, or a little later; but these are altogether the exception, forming, as it were, a local variety, and the Eastern characteristics therein displayed do not appear to have made further progress, even in France itself, until nearly the middle of the next century, when the Romanesque style was merging, or about to merge, into the Transitional. From that time examples rapidly multiplied, amongst them being capitals in the churches of St. Denis, St. Germain des Pres, Chartres, Sens, Notre Dame, Vézelay and Laon; and it may fairly be assumed that the great and comparatively sudden increase of Byzantinesque details at this time, about coinciding with the second great Crusade, was due, in large measure, to the increased knowledge of Eastern architecture brought about by the Holy Wars. The most typical specimens of Corinthianesque capital in England—those at Canterbury—were undeniably due to French influence, the architect coming to us straight from Sens and introducing work similar to, although a distinct advance upon, that at the French cathedral. Other English examples, *e.g.*, at Oakham Castle, Glastonbury, St. David's, etc., are considered to have been modelled upon those at Canterbury; but there are certainly many others—St. Cross and Bridlington, for example—which do not display the effects of French influence. Moreover, the French type itself, as I have above endeavoured to show, speedily developed here into pure Early English "stiff-leaved" foliage, a perfectly distinct type; the stems, ribs and veins of the acanthine and other Byzantinesque forms being directly modified into the stiff stalks rising from the neck of the capital which form so characteristic a feature of the thirteenth century English foliage. It is, however, a point of small moment for our purpose whether in particular instances the stimulus came through France, the important fact being that the source of the influence was the East, and the medium, to some extent, the Crusades.

In conclusion, I have to add a few more words as to the time and manner of introduction of the eastern ideas into this country. We have seen that the influence was exerted mainly in the twelfth century, that is to say, during the interval between the first and second Crusades and the period covered by the latter. The first Crusade resulted in the establishment of the Latin kingdom of Jerusalem, and during the whole of the twelfth century communications were constantly maintained between Syria and Western Europe by multitudes of warriors and pilgrims going and returning. Fresh bands of knights with their followers were constantly setting out for the Holy Land, whilst others, tired of fighting the Paynims and desiring once more to see their own homes and families, were returning. The fact of Palestine being in the hands of the Christians naturally afforded the visitors greatly increased facilities for observing and acquainting themselves at their leisure with the nature and details of the novelties, architectural or otherwise, around them—facilities the pilgrims for a long period before could not possibly have enjoyed, being allowed in the country only on sufferance. Although Englishmen took but a small part in the first Crusade, there were many amongst those who journeyed to the Holy Land in the succeeding (twelfth) century; and we know that the operations of the Crusaders were assisted by an English fleet at Jaffa in 1102, and again at Sidon in 1107. During the existence of the kingdom of Jerusalem many buildings—churches, castles, monasteries and private dwellings—were erected by the Crusaders in Syria, and these show evidence in some cases of the adoption of Byzantine and Saracenic ideas. Then one instance at least is recorded of a famous western architect (Eudes de Montreuil) being summoned to the seat of war to superintend the building of fortifications, and we may rest assured his mind would be opened to many new ideas that would bear fruit on his return.* So, no doubt, with others. The returning pilgrims and Crusaders carried with them portable objects of art as mementoes of their visit, such as woven materials, silks, tapestries, etc., illuminated MSS., and especially specimens of the carved ivory work—dyptiches, caskets, book-covers, and like objects—so characteristic of Byzantine art. These were very elaborately worked, and from them very many of the Byzantine ornamental details in our churches were derived. No one acquainted with the sculptured designs in some of our little village churches still possessing remnants of the original twelfth century work, who examines the ancient Byzantine ivories in the South Kensington Museum or other similar collections, can fail to be forcibly struck with the very close resemblance between the decorative details, in some cases amounting to absolute identity!

Although careful study and thought upon the subject of

---

* F. E. Hulme, *Birth and Development of Ornament.*

this paper have led me to believe that the influence, direct and indirect, of the Crusades upon English architecture was greater than I had previously held; yet, with the exception of one or two points upon which plain evidence is obtainable, the whole question resolves itself into a balancing of probabilities. Often when some certain result seems to have been reached further investigation shows qualification to be necessary, and not infrequently the qualification itself has to be qualified! Variations in the plan of our buildings, due to Eastern influence, were confined to a few special examples and had *no permanent* effect; but in many important matters of ornament and detail the influence appears to have been considerable and in some cases permanent. Although the whole effect exerted after 1096 by Eastern architecture upon our own cannot, for reasons assigned, be attributed to the Crusades, there seems little room for doubt that these formed by far the most powerful agent in the introduction, or in paving the way for the introduction, of ideas and methods which, although new here, were yet for the most part so ancient in the East.

JOSEPH W. BROOKES.

The British Record Society, Limited.

With which is Incorporated the Index Society.
Established 1878.

For Printing Calendars, Indexes, and Abstracts of British Records.

President:
The Most Noble the MARQUESS OF BUTE, K.T.

Chairman of Council:
G. E. COCKAYNE, Esq., M.A., F.S.A., *Norroy King of Arms.*

Hon. Treasurer:
GEORGE S. FRY, Esq., Inglewood, Walthamstow.

Hon. Secretary:
E. A. FRY, Esq., 172 Edmund Street, Birmingham.

The Society's Publications are contained in the "INDEX LIBRARY," which is issued quarterly.

The works completed include Chancery Proceedings *temp.* Charles I, Gloucestershire and London Inquisitiones post mortem and Calendars of Berkshire, Lichfield, Northamptonshire, Gloucestershire Wills, &c.

The works at present in course of publication include a complete Calendar of the Wills proved in the Prerogative Court of Canterbury, Calendars of Dorset Wills, Leicester Wills and Sussex Wills, and continuations of the London and Gloucester Inquisitiones post mortems, &c.

All communications and applications for the "INDEX LIBRARY" should be addressed to the Hon. Secretary, E. A. FRY, Esq., 172 Edmund Street, Birmingham.

CPSIA information can be obtained
at www.ICGtesting.com
Printed in the USA
BVHW040719230119
538277BV00046B/1282/P